YOSEMITE FALLS

an american icon

THE YOSEMITE FUND
IN COOPERATION WITH THE YOSEMITE ASSOCIATION
YOSEMITE NATIONAL PARK, CA

YOSEMITE ASSOCIATION

THE YOSEMITE FUND™
Providing for Yosemite's Future

Designed by DiVittorio & Associates,
San Francisco.

Published by the Yosemite Association,
P.O. Box 230, El Portal, CA 95318

Printed in Singapore.
ISBN-13: 978-1-930238-22-0

dedication

This book is dedicated to the many individuals and organizations who supported The Campaign for Yosemite Falls. More than 14,500 people contributed over $13.5 million to this multi-year effort, helping restore the once-trampled Lower Yosemite Fall area to a condition that complements the nobility and wonder of the falls themselves. The generosity of these individuals was invaluable and much appreciated. Thank you.

acknowledgments

Many people provided support and assistance to make this book possible. First and foremost, Bob Hansen of The Yosemite Fund consistently showed enthusiastic support for the book and shared his thoughtful insights and comprehensive library; his tireless dedication to Yosemite is extraordinary. Karen Sorensen authored the manuscript, diligently researching and culling feedback from Steve Medley of the Yosemite Association, former park historian Jim Snyder, Linda Eade of the Yosemite Research Library, and Barbara Beroza of the Yosemite Museum. Greg Cox of the Yosemite Slide Library and Miriam Luchans of the Yosemite Museum skillfully located and scanned historical images. Noted geologist N. King Huber provided a helpful review of the geological information. The Yosemite Association published the book, working on content and layout with the Fund's editor Lisa Lomba and graphic designer Dan DiVittorio.

the place

an american icon

*"I do not live 'near the Yosemite,' but in it —
in the very grandest warmest center of it.
I wish you could hear the Falls tonight —
they speak a most glorious language."*

John Muir, 1870

FOR MANY, John Muir's relationship to Yosemite and Yosemite Falls represents the ideal connection between man and nature. His rich, descriptive writing about Yosemite and his spiritual immersion in its landscape move many of us to venture there for a retreat from our daily lives. At the falls, the unmistakable feeling of serenity we experience stems from our connectedness to the natural world. The relationship between Yosemite Falls and the people who have been in their presence is reflected in their fascinating cultural history. This history expresses the desires of diverse individuals to foster an association or bond with one of the most awe-inspiring places on earth. The allure of the water, stone, and light at Yosemite Falls has infused with wonder those who have lived at its base, exploited its natural resources, climbed its trails and rocks, immortalized it in works of art, and finally protected it.

Visited and loved by thousands, the lower fall area became cluttered over time with a dilapidated blockhouse restroom, an overcrowded parking lot, and trails degraded from overuse. Between 1995 and 2005, this special place was converted into a more welcoming place with a stone amphitheatre, educational panels, wheelchair accessible trails, and sitting areas constructed of natural materials. In a joint effort, the National Park Service, The Yosemite Fund, Chevron volunteers, landscape architect Lawrence Halprin, and donors and volunteers spent countless hours and $13.5 million making these improvements to the base of the lower fall while protecting its natural landscape. The completed project exemplifies the respectful, balanced relationship that can exist between people and place.

Whether our interest is the cultural or natural history at the base of the lower fall or the natural drama at the precipice of the upper fall, Yosemite Falls challenges us to understand this landmark's past, to contemplate the prospects for its future, and to marvel at the humility, respect, and wonder with which it fills us.

(right) In winter, the falls provide a new spectacle—a delicate cascade adorned by patches of snow and ice.

(below) In spring, the powerful falls deliver a sweet mist to the surrounding rocks as well as hikers along the Upper Yosemite Falls trail.

Cook's Meadow boardwalk provides walkers with stunning views of the falls rising above the valley's black oaks and pine trees.

formation

"The finest photograph is utterly inadequate to convey to the mind any satisfactory impression…of how many of the elements of grandeur and beauty are combined in this waterfall."

J. D. Whitney, 1868

THE SOURCE OF YOSEMITE Falls lies close to the exact center of Yosemite National Park. Just north of 10,850-foot Mount Hoffmann, a stream called Yosemite Creek quietly begins. Soon joined by tributary streams, which feed and strengthen it, the creek makes its way some ten miles to the lip of Yosemite Valley, crashes to the valley floor where it merges with the Merced River, then flows many miles to the San Joaquin River before eventually reaching the ocean. While the water's plunge over Yosemite Falls is brief compared to the rest of its journey, it is spectacular, dropping almost 2,500 feet over the sheer, near-vertical upper wall of the valley, middle cascades, and lower fall. But it wasn't always so dramatic.

The Merced River, which runs through the center of Yosemite Valley, originally traversed gentle, rolling hills. Tensions in the Earth's crust forced the area now known as the Sierra Nevada to rise and tilt westward. As this uplift occurred, erosion increased and steeper slopes were formed. Tributary streams that fed the Merced River cascaded into a steeper-walled canyon, the predecessor of today's Yosemite Valley. During the Ice Age, glaciers formed in the high Sierra, a number of which descended through the Merced River Canyon. At least one of these glaciers filled the Yosemite Valley area completely, covering some of its domes.

As the glaciers passed through, they scraped away the soil and scoured the bedrock floor of the valley, carving into the lower channels of the tributary streams and leaving them steeper than before. As a result, the upper sections of the tributary streams, such as Bridalveil Creek, were left in "hanging valleys" with the streams dropping as waterfalls high above the valley. As a result of this process, Yosemite Valley today contains some of the highest waterfalls on Earth.

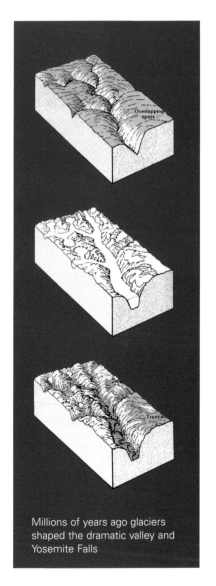

Millions of years ago glaciers shaped the dramatic valley and Yosemite Falls

The falls' brushy ledges formed by horizontal joints are best viewed by hikers along the Upper Yosemite Falls trail's numerous switchbacks, shown on the left.

Some geologists believe that the origin of Yosemite Falls is slightly different from that of other waterfalls in the valley, and that Yosemite Creek once descended into the valley through a deep ravine just west of the current falls. There, an ancient streambed still can be observed both above the valley rim and below it. Evidence suggests that this remained the path of Yosemite Creek even after major glaciers passed through Yosemite Valley.

Some geologists theorize that the creek's original course was altered by the moraines created by later, smaller glaciers that flowed down the Yosemite Creek basin. The present position of Yosemite Creek allows it to make a much more dramatic leap from the hanging valley, plummeting 1,430 feet over the precipitous cliff to the cascades below.

The water's dramatic descent is also shaped by horizontal joints in the cliffs framing Yosemite Falls. These are marked by brushy ledges at the bottom of the upper fall and at the top of the lower fall, the latter known as Sunnyside Bench. These joints created the relatively flat stretch of rock over which the falls run between the much steeper upper and lower falls.

The rock surface behind and beneath Yosemite Falls is still changing. While the lower portions of the cliff—where more mist accumulates, freezes, and thaws—are eroding more rapidly, the granite next to the upper fall is comparatively stable. Still, pressure within the cliff slowly causes exfoliating slabs of rock to form parallel to the surface. In November, 1980, a 270-foot granite slab weighing about 4,400 tons fell on the Yosemite Falls Trail just west of the upper fall. Lost Arrow Spire, a large detached column of rock near Yosemite Falls, is a remnant of another of these slabs.

season cycle

So long a column of water and spray is swayed from side to side by the wind…the resistance of the rocks at the top, and of the air in the whole descent, produces a billowy motion. The combination of these two motions, both so conspicuous in this fall, is inexpressibly graceful."

Joseph LeConte, 1875

YOSEMITE FALLS ARE AT THEIR HEIGHT IN SPRING when melting winter snow collected within the watershed of Yosemite Creek forms a torrent that plunges over the cliffs into the valley. The avalanche of water fills the rock basin with spray and often turbulent wind. Rainbows appear and disappear, and the thundering sound of the falls reverberates throughout the valley and rattles windows at Yosemite Lodge.

The effect of the wind on this rush of water can be magical. Thomas Starr King, noted author and minister, elegantly described the wind's work in 1860:

"What endless complexities and opulence of beauty in the forms and motions of the cataract!…[T]he most charming fretwork of watery nodules, each trailing its vapory train for a hundred feet, or more, is woven all over the cascade, which swings, now and then, thirty feet each way on the mountain side, as if it were a pendulum of watery lace. Once in a while, too, the wind manages to get back of the fall, between it and the cliff, and then it will whirl it round and round for two or three hundred feet."

By late summer, the falls become a mere trickle, and they often dry up entirely by autumn, when the nearby oak, dogwood, and maple trees are awash in vibrant color and the granite's dark markings trace the water's seasonal path.

In spring, the falls are at their height.

"[The] frozen spray gives rise to one of the most interesting winter features of the Valley — a cone of ice at the foot of the fall, four or five hundred feet high."

John Muir, 1912

Winter at the falls presents other unique phenomena. "Every clear, frosty morning loud sounds are heard booming and reverberating from side to side of the Valley," John Muir wrote. "The strange thunder is made by the fall of sections of ice formed of spray that is frozen on the face of the cliff along the sides of the Upper Yosemite Fall...This frozen spray gives rise to one of the most interesting winter features of the Valley—a cone of ice at the foot of the fall, four or five hundred feet high."

During most years the cone doesn't reach more than 250 feet in height, but it occasionally attains greater size. In 1937, the

In fall, the falls are reduced to a trickle with their tracks etched darkly in the granite.

In winter, the falls become an opaque wonderland, accenting the cliff's indentations in white and creating a 250-foot snowcone at the base of Upper Yosemite Fall.

Yosemite Creek flows determinedly under the old Yosemite Falls Bridge.

park service engineering department at Yosemite surveyed the ice cone, and extrapolating from its results, estimated the size of a particularly large cone that appeared in a photo dating from Muir's time. The engineers found that cone to be 322 feet high. Its base covered an area of 3.7 acres and the structure contained more than 25 million cubic feet of ice and snow.

Once temperatures warm in early spring, water from the upper fall begins to penetrate the top of the cone, creating a volcano-like structure, and by mid-April, most of the cone has melted. While ice cones form at the base of other Yosemite waterfalls, none are as impressive as the Yosemite Falls ice cone.

Another winter occurrence in and around Yosemite Falls is frazil ice, a slushy, milky substance that forms in the falls and the creek below. When a period of warmer weather is followed by a sudden drop in temperature, turbulence and rapid freezing cause ice crystals to form in the water and group together in spongy masses. These masses sometimes overflow the creek bed, changing the course of the stream. Frazil ice below the falls in Yosemite Creek has sometimes reached a depth of more than twenty feet, covering trails and bridges and even flowing through buildings that once bordered the creek. In 1953, a large flow covered nearly forty acres in the area.

the people

the legend of chó-lock

the ahwahneechee

LONG BEFORE YOSEMITE became known to the world, Yosemite Falls featured prominently in the lives of Yosemite Indians, the Ahwahneechee, whose occupation of the valley may go back more than 4,000 years. These Native Americans called the waterfall "Chó-lock," meaning "the fall." At one time, there were over thirty-five different Indian villages and campsites in Yosemite Valley, but just below the waterfall was the largest and most important village, "Koom-í-ne," extending for three-quarters of a mile along the base of the cliff. There, beside a large oak tree, the renowned Chief Tenaya had an earth-covered ceremonial house (a "hang-e").

The Ahwahneechee, composed of largely Southern Sierra Miwok-speaking people (later joined by Mono Lake Paiute), lived in Yosemite Valley and depended on the land for sustenance. They spent much of their time gathering food, including seeds, berries, and bulbs, and hunting for deer, birds, and other animals. The Ahwahneechee were expert basket makers, and like other California Native Americans, they relied heavily on acorns. Oak trees were plentiful in the valley, and each fall's acorn harvest was both stored and ground to make acorn mush and bread. Grinding stones, still visible today, mark the sites of this activity near the base of Lower Yosemite Fall.

The Ahwahneechee told various myths and legends, many of which related to the astounding natural scenery that surrounded them. El Capitan was known as "Tu-tok-a-nu'-la," named after a measuring worm that saved two bear cubs that were stranded on top of the massive rock. Half Dome was "Tis-se'-yak," the name of a young woman who, along with her husband, was turned into stone by the gods after the two quarreled.

Myths also told of water spirits that resided in Yosemite's waterfalls. Not all of these spirits were friendly. One story about Yosemite Falls describes a group of spirits, known as the "Po'-loti," that lived in the waters near the base of the great waterfall.

Native American woman processes acorns for eating.

Frederick Butman, *Yosemite Falls,* oil on canvas, 1859. This is the earliest surviving full-scale depiction of Yosemite by a professional artist.

In the waters just below Cho'-lok (Yosemite Falls) live the Po'-loti, a group of dangerous spirit women. In the old days there was a village a short distance from the falls.

A maiden from this village went to the stream for a basket of water. She dipped the basket into the stream as usual, but brought it up full of snakes.

She went farther up stream and tried again, but with the same result. She tried repeatedly, each time a little farther up stream, but always drew a basketful of snakes. Finally, she reached the pool at the foot of Cho'-lok, and a sudden, violent wind blew her into it.

During the night she gave birth to a child, which she

wrapped in a blanket and brought home the next morning. The girl's mother was very curious and soon took the blanket off the baby in order to see it.

Immediately a violent gale arose and blew the entire village and its inhabitants into this same pool. Nothing has ever been seen or heard of them since.

others discover the waterfall

"The surging roll of music from this fall is a constant and refreshing lullaby to slumber, and never wearies."

James Hutchings, 1886

THE FIRST NON-INDIANS to see Yosemite Falls were members of the Mariposa Battalion, which entered Yosemite Valley in 1851. Around this time, pioneers and gold miners in the Mariposa area were advancing further into territory traditionally occupied by Native Americans, and skirmishes between the two groups were on the rise. The battalion was dispatched to Yosemite Valley, the rumored home of a resistive band of Indians, with the intent of capturing the Ahwahnee-chee there. The group, led by local trading post operator James D. Savage, was at first unsuccessful in its effort. Because the Ahwahnee-chee fled before the battalion arrived, Savage had the battalion burn the many food stores he found in the Indian villages. Subsequent trips made the same year, however, resulted in the capture of the Native Americans still residing in the valley.

While most of the battalion remained fixed on its mission of routing out Indians, one member, a young private named Lafayette Bunnell, was charmed by the Yosemite Valley and began naming its natural wonders. After describing how he and his fellows had named the valley "Yosemite," Bunnell wrote about how the name Yosemite Falls came to be.

"[Since the fall]…appeared to be the principal one of the Sierras… I gave it the name of 'Yosemite Falls,' and in so naming it I but followed out the idea of the Indians who called it 'Choo-Look' …which signifies…'The Fall.'"

The account of the battalion's trips was not widely known, but James Mason Hutchings, a gold

Stereoscopic view of the Agassiz Column and Yosemite Falls.

(left) Tourist party at Yosemite Falls, 1896.

(clockwise from upper left) The first photograph of Yosemite by Charles Weed; John Muir; the Hutchings Sawmill with "Hang Nest;" and James Hutchings' home.

Stone lithograph of Thomas Ayres' drawing of Yosemite Falls, 1855, the first published picture of Yosemite.

seeker turned journalist and promoter from England, read a printed article about the excursions. He was particularly captivated by the mention of a thousand-foot waterfall, which was prime material for his planned illustrated monthly about California. In the summer of 1855, he and three other men (including a hired artist named Thomas Ayres) comprised the first "tourist" party to visit Yosemite Valley. The group, led by local Indian guides, spent a few days absorbing the magnificent scenery, while Hutchings took extensive notes and Ayres made sketches.

Hutchings' subsequent newspaper article for the local *Mariposa Gazette* began to spread the word about Yosemite. Later that year, a lithograph of Ayres' drawing of Yosemite Falls was published, and the world was exposed to the first modern Yosemite image. In 1859 Hutchings returned to Yosemite, this time with the pioneer landscape photographer, Charles L. Weed. Weed's picture of Yosemite Falls was the first photograph ever taken in Yosemite.

Several other published accounts of Yosemite Valley soon appeared throughout the country, written by such notables as *New York Tribune* editor Horace Greeley and the popular minister and author Thomas Starr King. At the same time, Yosemite images created by another photographer, Carleton E. Watkins (among them beautiful mammoth-plate prints of Yosemite Falls) were frequently exhibited in New York. Not surprisingly, more tourists began coming to the valley. The vaunted Yosemite Falls were largely what attracted these early visitors, despite the difficult and dangerous trip on foot and horseback required at the time.

Camping near the base of Yosemite Falls.

tourism and preservation begin

*"I rode back to the hotel and thence to the foot of the Yosemite Falls …
there is very little talking there. The common expressions of wonder,
surprise, admiration or pleasure are not often heard. Men and women gaze
and are silent and even little children are made quiet by the overwhelming
majesty of the place."*

Rev. J. M. Buckley, D.D., 1883

JAMES HUTCHINGS' newspaper and magazine articles of the late 1850s helped spawn tourism in Yosemite, and Hutchings recognized a potentially lucrative career opportunity as a hotel proprietor. In 1864 he bought the Upper Hotel, one of the first hotels in Yosemite Valley, and moved there with his family to run it. He quickly became Yosemite's primary promoter. In an interesting historical twist, he hired John Muir to run a sawmill powered by the water of Yosemite Creek that flowed from the base of Yosemite Falls. Muir built and operated the mill, cutting boards from trees that had fallen in previous winter storms to provide lumber to upgrade the hotel.

Hutchings' acclaim for Yosemite Falls and his promotion of the valley as a wonderful tourist destination with hotels conflicted with Muir's romantic desire, expressed in his writings, for people to return to and be transformed by nature. But by hiring Muir and providing him with housing in the valley, Hutchings allowed Muir to develop as a legendary spokesman for greater Yosemite and its preservation.

Though profit was Hutchings' motivation for living in and encouraging others to come to the valley, he did possess an earnest affection for Yosemite Valley and its famous falls, expressed in his descriptive, prolific writing. Here, he describes the Yosemite

Falls in an 1877 tourist guide: "It seems such a luxury to lie awake and listen to the splashing, washing, roaring, surging, hissing, seething sound of the great Yo Semite Falls, just opposite; or to pass quietly out of our resting-place…to watch, in the moonlight, the ever-changing shapes of the water as it leaps the cloud-draped summit of the mountain and falls in gusty torrents on the unyielding granite, to be dashed to an infinity of atoms."

Despite their shared aesthetic appreciation of Yosemite, Muir and Hutchings often found themselves at odds. Muir expressed disdain for the kind of superficial tourism Hutchings and his hotel promoted. In a letter he wrote,

YOSEMITE NATIONAL PARK

319 NEVADA FALLS   YOSEMITE FALLS   VERNAL FALLS   BRIDAL VEIL FALLS

24

YOSEMITE FALLS, IN WINTER, YOSEMITE VALLEY, CALIF.

YOSEMITE FALLS, a lithograph of the water color painting from the brush of Gunnar Widforss.

The Head Waiter will be glad to furnish, without charge, copies of this menu to guests who care to have them as Souvenirs. Envelopes to fit are available for those who care to mail them to friends.

CAMP CURRY

July 2, 1926

LUNCHEON

Sour Pickles

Consommé Gelée   Manhattan Clam Chowder

Choice of

Filet of Sole, Tartar Sauce
Hungarian Goulash with Spatzen
Braised Shoulder of Veal, Kidney Beans
Combination Vegetable Dinner, Poached Egg

Baked Summer Squash au Fromage   Hashed Potatoes

Hearts of Lettuce, Green Peppers, French Dressing

Cherry Pie   Grape Nut Custard, Cream Sauce
Raspberry Ice, Lemon Cookies

Corn Bread
White, Raisin and Rye Bread

Tea   Coffee   Chocolate   Milk   Iced Tea

Breakfast 6:00-8:45 a. m. Lunch 12-2 p. m. Dinner 5:30-8 p. m.

Y T S SADDLE TRIPS

While you are in Yosemite, you will hear the Old Timers talking of a mythical land known as "the back country". The back country is no longer mythical to those who have seen Yosemite by means of the YTS saddle trips. All through the 1125 square miles of Yosemite National Park are well kept trails winding past meadows, Sierra peaks, lakes, trout streams, glaciers, forests and mountain passes. The Yosemite Transportation System has horses specially trained for mountain trails. YTS saddle trips are made under the escort of competent and popular guides who know the Yosemite Sierras. The man at the transportation office will be pleased to give you details regarding YTS saddle trips.

"The tide of visitors will float slowly about the bottom of the valley as a harmless scum, collecting in hotel and saloon eddies, leaving the rocks and falls eloquent as ever and instinct with imperishable beauty and greatness."

Muir imagined the tourist on a spiritual quest that might not always be a conscious one:

"The regular tourist, ever on the flow, is one of the most characteristic productions of the present century; and however frivolous and inappreciative the poorer specimens may appear, viewed comprehensively they are a most hopeful and significant sign of the times, indicating at least the beginning of our return to nature…

Men, women and children of every creed and color come here from every nation…the so-called high and low, titled and obscure, all in some degree seeing and loving fresh, wild beauty, and traveling to better purpose than they know, borne onward like ships at sea by currents they cannot understand."

As publicity about Yosemite increased, concern grew about the long-term protection of Yosemite Valley and the nearby Mariposa Grove of Big Trees. A group of prominent citizens formed to advance the idea of preserving these resources for the public good. A key individual in the effort was Israel Ward Raymond, the California represen-

tative of a New York steamship transit company. Raymond, described by one historian as a public-spirited citizen, had visited Yosemite Valley and become concerned about its private exploitation.

In 1864 Raymond wrote a letter to Senator John Conness in Washington urging that Yosemite Valley and the Mariposa Grove be granted to the State of California "for public use, resort and recreation and (be) inalienable forever." Along with the letter, Raymond included several of Carleton E. Watkins' impressive large-format photographs of Yosemite, which likely included images of Yosemite Falls he took in the early 1860s.

The Hutchings Hotel, c. 1870.

The first visitors arrived on foot and horseback to see Yosemite Falls (1879).

efforts of John Muir, who advocated that Yosemite's watersheds in their entirety be protected. After two Muir articles and hand-drawn maps delineating boundaries for the "Watershed of Yosemite Valley" appeared in *Century Magazine* in 1890, the bill was passed establishing Yosemite National Park and extending protection to some 1,500 square miles, including all of the rivers and streams flowing into the valley. Because the National Park Service had not yet been created, U.S. Cavalry troops from San Francisco were sent to the park each summer to enforce laws, patrol the trails, and provide general oversight.

Shortly thereafter Conness introduced a bill to preserve Yosemite and the Mariposa Grove. The bill passed both houses of Congress, and the Yosemite Grant was signed by President Abraham Lincoln in the midst of the Civil War. This action — the first time a natural area had been preserved by a federal government — formed the foundation of a new and important concept: the national park system. While Yellowstone became the first official national park in 1872, the 1864 Yosemite Grant is viewed by many to have originated the national park idea.

Once stage roads were built to Yosemite in 1874 and the economic depression of the mid- to late-1870s passed, tourism increased and even more people came to view Yosemite and its famous waterfalls. Rather than descend the last several miles into Yosemite Valley on horseback down a steep, dangerous trail, visitors could now travel in comparatively comfortable stagecoaches.

In 1890 the large area surrounding the valley was set aside as a national park, largely due to the

Yosemite Valley and the Mariposa Grove continued to be administered by the State of California until 1906, when responsibility for these areas was transferred to the federal government. The U.S. Army troops that had been stationed in Wawona then moved their headquarters into

Camp Yosemite, summer 1909.

the valley. The area near the base of Lower Yosemite Fall, at that time still inhabited by Native Americans, was turned into a camp for the troops. Over time, a number of structures, including stables, barracks, kitchens, headquarters office, and a hospital were built at the camp, which existed in the present-day Yosemite Lodge area until 1915.

After the army camp was discontinued, Joseph Desmond leased the site and converted it to visitor lodging, eventually building over one hundred redwood cabins, a swimming pool, and other structures to accommodate the increasing number of tourists. When automobiles became the preferred form of transportation, the first all-year highway into

Playing golf at the Ahwahnee Hotel with Yosemite Falls in the background.

Yosemite opened in 1926. In 1956 Yosemite Lodge was rebuilt in the same location to meet the demands of even greater numbers of visitors that traveled to Yosemite after World War II.

Today, Yosemite Falls remain the quintessential experience for many visitors — each year nearly one million people come to the base of the falls to view what is now a world renowned icon.

Ahwahneechee Indians, entrepreneurs like Hutchings and Desmond, Galen Clark, John Muir, tourists, the U.S. Army — these diverse groups and individuals dramatically changed the falls landscape with their personal and professional interests and lives, transforming the area, for better or worse. Their central roles in the falls story and their ideological differences draw attention to the thorny questions we face as we coexist with nature: how do we respectfully balance our simultaneous desire for civilized comforts with our need to be a part of the natural world?

The old parking lot at Yosemite Falls where an amphitheatre now exists.

"The Falls are now at their middle volume of water, beautiful as ever, whitening as they make their careless leap over the great perpendicular height, widening and involving into a thousand magical and fantastic forms of beauty; silvery falling rocks and meteors, softening into folds of lace and misty gauze ever disappearing into the cauldron of water and spray beneath."

Galen Clark, 1868

yosemite falls—a "humbug"

Among the more well-known Yosemite tourists in 1859 was Horace Greeley, editor of the *New York Tribune*. After a strenuous horseback ride on "one of the hardest trotting horses in America," Greeley arrived in Yosemite Valley tired and uncomfortable. While he was enamored of the valley as a whole, he later pronounced Yosemite Falls a "humbug" and a mere "trout brook." Greeley visited in August, after the spring snow melt had ceased and the falls had nearly dried up. The disappointment of late-summer and fall tourists may have contributed to a proposal in the early 1900s to dam Yosemite Creek above the upper fall, allowing a regulated year-round flow of water over the falls. The idea was ultimately rejected, leaving the Yosemite Falls in their natural state of beauty.

Chris Jorgensen, *Yosemite Falls and Overhanging Rock,* watercolor on paper, date unknown.

people and place

yosemite falls by foot

"Therefore we are all, in some sense, mountaineers, and going to the mountains is going home."

John Muir, 1898

"We push on until the top of the Falls is reached. A great shout bursts from our throats spontaneously . . . we bare our heads to the spray. The water dashes against the rocks with such force as to divide it into tiny shot, each shot a diamond, when the sun is not turning them into jasper, amethyst, and gold."

Dr. Cora A. Morse, 1896

WHILE TOURISTS annually flock to the viewpoint at the base of Lower Yosemite Fall, a much smaller number hike to the very top of the falls or scale the granite walls that serve as their backdrop.

The long, strenuous Yosemite Falls trail was constructed over 125 years ago by John Conway, who built and formalized other early Yosemite trails. Completed in 1877, the trail was operated as a toll route until 1885, when Conway sold it to the State of California for $1,500.

Today's hiker can follow the trail free of charge starting from where it begins near Camp 4, the historic climbers' camp, just west of Yosemite Lodge. It switchbacks up through shaded forest, then breaks out into the open for a panoramic view of Yosemite Valley at Columbia Rock (2 miles round trip; 1,000 feet of elevation gain). The trail then horizontally traverses a long bench until it turns a corner, revealing a spec-tacular first view of the entire upper fall. The route then descends briefly into the basin and ascends a gully to the left of the fall, climbing steeply along more than 80 switchbacks (there are 135 in all) until reaching the lip of Upper Yosemite Fall (7.2 miles round-trip; 2,700 feet of elevation gain). At the rim a stairway leads to a railed viewpoint that offers a sublime view of Yosemite Creek as it flies off the granite crest and plummets down a sheer cliff to the valley below.

Rarer vistas of the Yosemite Falls can be had by the climber. Lost Arrow Spire, a large, narrow column of rock that juts out from the cliff near the upper fall, was the location of one of the early first-ascents in the valley, as well as the first "big wall" climb in Yosemite. In September of 1946, Jack Arnold, Robin Hansen, Fritz Lippmann, and Anton Nelson successfully completed a spectacular "aerial traverse" between the Yosemite Valley rim and the tip of the spire. Through a series of rope feats, including the toss of a lasso over the top of the spire, Jack Arnold became the first man to stand atop Lost Arrow Spire. One year later, Anton Nelson and Salathé spent five days and nights climbing the spire from a point near the base of Upper Yosemite Fall, completing the first big wall climb; until then, no one had spent more than a single night on the rock face.

"After the second day our muscles no longer cramped and we

Climbers atop Lost Arrow Spire.

"Just why is Yosemite climbing so different? The basic reason lies in the rock itself. Nowhere else in the world is the rock so exfoliated, so glacier-polished and so devoid of handholds... Special techniques and equipment have evolved through absolute necessity."

Yvon Chouinard, 1963

Climber Ron Kauk scales one of the many climbing routes near Yosemite Falls.

the vestibule

"The Vestibule—a long, broad passage behind the falls…is a curiosity of itself; when a heavy stream is pouring over, the scene is indescribable. You can see up behind the water several hundred feet a wreathing mass. The water falls in volumes, for a moment it appears to slacken or shut off; then a massive torrent comes with a crash and a loud explosive noise; at times a loud hum or buzzing noise is heard, similar to that of the fan blast of a furnace; you feel an exhilarating influence from inhaling the compressed atmosphere; you witness all the elements of a raging tempest at sea without feeling the unpleasant sense of fear or danger. When a light stream is falling, you can enjoy that most brilliant play of the imagination, a shimmering sheet of diamonds. In the four years last past, the writer has entered the Vestibule hundreds of times, accompanied by timid ladies and gentlemen, and never encountered any risk or danger whatever. The only discomfort is when the wind carries the column westward. The spray is like a heavy rain."

John Conway

put thirst in its place," Nelson later wrote of his adventure with Salathé. "Bivouacking on the chockstones with our feet dangling, our backs aching where they were being nudged by granite knobs, and our shoulders tugging at their anchors, we got little sleep. Cold winds barely permitted us to keep warm enough for the rest essential to the digestion of food…food, sleep, and water can be dispensed with to a degree not appreciated until one is in a position where little can be had."

Each year, hundreds of climbers come to Yosemite to scale the park's famous big walls, including those near Yosemite Falls. The climbing routes can be challenging, a fact exemplified by their names, such as Wheel of Torture, World of Pain, and Dante's Inferno. Camp 4, at the base of the Yosemite Falls Trail, is still known as the climbers' camp, and Lost Arrow Spire, along with several other charted climbs along the walls beneath Yosemite Falls, remains a popular destination.

John Conway, the nineteenth-century builder and operator of a toll trail to the top of Yosemite Falls, wrote about a hidden passage behind the upper fall in an 1881 trail guide. The chamber provided hardier tourists with an extreme close-up of the waterfall's majestic power.

Thomas Hill, *Yosemite Falls,* oil on canvas, 1883.

the artist's view

VISITORS CAN LEARN how the Yosemite Falls were formed from the writings of geologists and historians. Hiking and climbing the falls, on the other hand, provide powerful, direct, intimate interactions with them. Artists who attempt to depict Yosemite Falls have the two-fold task of informing and inspiring the viewer or reader. Their representations need to evoke the place, while ideally capturing the ephemeral, mysterious qualities that draw us to the landscape. Combining color, clarity, and texture, poets, writers, painters, and photographers bring the fleeting experience of Yosemite Falls into permanence.

Over the years many artists have captured the falls in poetry, prose, painting, drawing, and photography, and contemporary artists continue to be captivated by their wonder. From the original sketches of Thomas Ayres to Carleton Watkins' amazing mammoth plates to the works of Wallace Stegner and Gary Snyder, artists have helped us see all facets of Yosemite Falls — its natural formation, its history, and the uniqueness that continues to enthrall us today.

Carleton Watkins, *Yosemite Falls (River View 2,477 ft.)*, 1861.

the yosemite

Yet I know it is real,
    for I see the spray
Of Yosemite Fall in
    the moonlight play,
Swaying and trembling—
    a radiant glow,
From the sky above
    to the vale below;
Like the ladder of old
    to Jacob given,
A line of light from
    earth to heaven.

Wallace Bruce, 1880

Linda Abbott, *Yosemite Falls,* oil on canvas, 2001.

Gunnar Widforss, *Yosemite Falls,* watercolor, circa 1920.

cloud mist

YOSEMITE FALLS

A burst of molten silver, born
    Of mountain snow,
That bears the beauty of the morn
    Within its flow.

A wave of streaming white that falls,
    And, falling, flings
Against the gray old granite walls
    Its silver wings.

A whitened fire from out the sky,
    Whose arrowed strands
In sunlight gleam and flash and die,
    Like earth-hurled brands.

A rush, as surges of the sea,
    That, dashing, wakes
Dull echoes of a musketry
    Where'er it breaks.

A river turned to cloud mist, blown
    By every breath,
Yet coming to its crystal own,
    After death.

Harold Symmes, 1911

falls

Over stone lip
    the creek leaps out as one
    divides in spray and streamers,
    lets it all: go,

Above, back there, the snowfields,
    rocked between granite ribs
    turn spongy in the summer sun
    water slips out under
    mucky shallow flows
    enmeshed with roots of flower & moss & heather
    seeps through swampy meadow
    gathers to shimmer sandy shiny flats
    then soars off ledges—

Crash and thunder on the boulders at the base.
    painless, playing,
    droplets regather
    seek the lowest, and keep going down.
    in gravelly beds.

There is no use, the water cycle tumbles round—

Annette Bottaro-Walklet, *Upper Yosemite Falls*,
color photograph, 1996.

Sierra Nevada
    could lift the heart so high
    fault block uplift
    thrust of westward slipping crust—one way
    to raise and swing the clouds around—
    thus pine trees leapfrog up on sunlight
    trapped in cells of leaf—
    nutrient minerals called together
    like a magic song
    to lead a cedar log along, that hopes
        to get to sea at last, a great canoe,

A soft breath, world-wide, of night and day.
    rising, falling,

The Great Mind passes by its own
    fine-honed thoughts,
    going each way.

Rainbow hanging steady
    only slightly wavering with the
    swing of the whole spill
        between the rising and the falling,
            stands still.

I stand drenched in crashing spray and mist,
        and pray.

                     Gary Snyder, late 1970s

Chiura Obata, *Evening Glow at Yosemite Falls*,
color woodblock print, 1930.

BEFORE

(clockwise from upper left) Supporters gather at new approach to celebrate the Yosemite Falls project; one of four reconstructed bridges; the approach to Lower Yosemite Fall; and the raised boardwalk on the Yosemite Falls Loop Trail protects fragile habitat. (center) Before the restoration.

the yosemite falls project

BETWEEN 1995 AND 2005 The Yosemite Fund, the National Park Service, and landscape architect Lawrence Halprin combined their talents to transform the dilapidated area around Lower Yosemite Fall and to restore a measure of natural beauty to a location that draws so many people each year. To complete this renovation, $13.5 million were generously and jointly provided by over 14,500 Friends of Yosemite, with assistance form the National Park Service.

During his sixty-year career, renowned landscape architect Lawrence Halprin has authored books that feature his sketches and thoughts on the relationship of people and environment, received countless awards for his work, and had his designs exhibited at the San Francisco Museum of Modern Art. He is known for transforming cold urban landscapes into places of natural beauty with the right combinations of stones, water, and plant life.

The *San Francisco Chronicle* reported in May, 2005, "If there is an urban monument built of stone with water flowing through it, it was probably put there by Halprin." Such projects by Halprin include Ghirardelli Square and Levi's Plaza in San Francisco, the Lovejoy and Auditorium Forecourt Plazas in Portland, Freeway Park in Seattle, the FDR Memorial in Washington, D.C., and the Haas Promenade in Jerusalem.

A 1992 article written about the Yosemite Falls area prior to its redesign noted: "From the fume-ridden parking lots, where the diesels of the tour buses are left roaring to keep the air conditioners going, it is about… a ten-minute walk down a miserable blacktop path to the ugly joke of a bridge that crosses the creek beneath the falls." The walking path resembled a chopped-off road more than a trail, and the overcrowded, noisy, polluted parking lot was a distraction from the natural splendor and powerful sounds of the Merced River and the lower fall. With paltry wayside signs, a severely dilapidated concrete-block restroom facility, no place to sit down, and no other amenities, the area saw visitors unintentionally trampling the forest floor, chaining bikes to trees, and changing baby diapers in the woods.

One can only wonder what Halprin's thoughts might have been as he stood at the foot of the Lower Yosemite Fall in 1996, in an area whose beauty, already defined by water, stone, and light, had been compromised over time. Halprin observed: "I couldn't change the landscape. The falls are there. What I could do was rework the bridge, redesign some of the trails."

The new shuttle bus stop.

the natural and cultural landscape. The measures taken to safeguard the Yosemite Falls area were extensive and included the following:

- Archeological assessors ensured that no historical artifacts were eliminated by the project construction;

- Native Americans monitored the site throughout construction, watching for artifacts;

- No stones from the park were quarried for the project. Almost all were recycled from other areas in the park, including the curb wall of the Arch Rock Road;

- Granite dust from construction was vacuumed to protect air and water quality;

- The main bridge was diapered to prevent oil-infused asphalt from entering the water;

- The old asphalt from the parking lot was hauled out of the park for use as road base;

- Trees were wrapped for protection during construction, and streambeds were fenced; and

- New machinery was purchased for all construction to prevent any potential leaks.

In the summer of 1997, The Yosemite Fund and the National Park Service sponsored two workshops with about thirty-five people in each, conducted by Halprin. Among this group were diverse representatives of the National Park Service, the Sierra Club, the American Alpine Club, tour bus operators, wheelchair users, and several others from various organizations with relationships to the park.

For the first workshop Halprin created workbooks for participants to record their thoughts and impressions during guided explorations of the area. He collected and analyzed these thoughts and comments, and a final workshop was held to develop the group's consensus about transforming the lower fall area.

Using the workshop results, Halprin created the conceptual design and plans for construction. In 1999 the project became part of the larger Valley Implementation Plan. Over the next nine years Halprin's design was augmented, edited, and implemented through dedicated collaboration between the National Park Service, Halprin's office, The Yosemite Fund, donors, engineers, contractors, and subcontractors.

Construction in a national park setting presents unique challenges, particularly in protecting

(clockwise from upper left) Visitors use new roadside map; perched on new dry-laid stone wall, a young visitor enjoys the sun; Yosemite Fund President Bob Hansen, National Park Service Director Fran Mainella, and Superintendent Mike Tollefson at the dedication; a ranger and mountaineer Mark Wellman enjoy a stroll along one of several new raised boardwalks; granite-based exhibits help visitors navigate the area; and, a multi-use trail lined with boulders and dry-laid stone walls defines the new approach.

The extraordinary combination of funding, visionary planning, and careful construction that came together for the Yosemite Falls project testifies to the purposeful, successful work that can be achieved when diverse constituents work cooperatively. During the span of the project, the following improvements were made to the lower fall area:

Visitors walk over the reconstructed Yosemite Falls Bridge.

- Creation of a handicapped accessible trail to the viewing plaza and main bridge that meets Americans with Disabilities Act (ADA) standards;

- Expansion of the main viewing plaza at the base of the lower fall;

- Reconstruction of four bridges, removal of two bridges, and construction of one new bridge and two new boardwalks over sensitive habitat;

- Installation of ten educational exhibits, four orientation maps, one bronze relief map, and new directional signs throughout the area;

- Demolition of the old bathroom, restoration of the site, and development of an amphitheatre;

- Habitat restoration throughout the fifty-two acres, including repair of trampled stream banks and elimination of abandoned trails;

- Removal of the asphalt parking lot, followed by revegetation of the area;

- Construction of a new restroom and shuttle bus stop;

- Construction of a picnic area; and

- Installation of amenities including a drinking fountain, bike racks, trash and recycling receptacles, public telephone, and log benches.

The project was completed on time and on budget in December of 2004. The official dedication of the Yosemite Falls project took place on April 18, 2005, and coincided with the start of Earth Week. Sponsored by Chevron, KPIX Channel 5, and Delaware North Companies Parks and Resorts at Yosemite, the ceremony and reception honored all those whose participation made the project a success. Over 700 special guests witnessed the placement of the final granite boulder and walked the new paths to the foot of the falls.

In addition to being an amazing collaboration, this project demonstrates that preservation and use can be balanced. Neither the essential needs of people nor the integrity of the natural habitat was significantly compromised in order to accomplish the makeover of the Yosemite Falls area. While the length, required funding, and scope of this project were considerable, the spectacular, serene environment that now characterizes the lower fall area is certainly justification.

The desire of visitors to immerse themselves in the Yosemite Falls landscape has grown with the restoration of the area's natural beauty and function. After the project's completion, National Park Service Director Fran Mainella wrote, "I truly believe the Yosemite Falls Project represents a model partnership that has set an example for all the Park Service."

bibliography

Badè, William Frederic. *The Life and Letters of John Muir.* Vol. 1. Boston: Houghton Mifflin Co., 1924.

Browning, Peter. *John Muir in His Own Words.* Lafayette, Calif.: Great West Books, 1988.

———. *Yosemite Place Names.* 2d ed. Lafayette, Calif.: Great West Books, 2005.

Bruce, Wallace. *The Yosemite.* Boston: Lee and Shepard; New York: Charles T. Dillingham, 1880.

Buckley, Rev. J. M. *Two Weeks in the Yosemite and Vicinity.* New York: Phillips & Hunt, 1883.

Bunnell, Lafayette Houghton. *Discovery of the Yosemite and the Indian War of 1851 Which Led to That Event.* Reprint of 1911 edition. Yosemite: Yosemite Association, 1990.

Conway, John. *Tourists' Guide from the Yosemite Valley to Eagle Peak, for the spring and summer of 1881.* San Francisco: C. W. Nevin & Co., 1881.

Ernst, Emil F. "He Brought Yosemite to the World." *Yosemite Nature Notes* 35 (July 1956): 116-117.

Greeley, Horace. *An Overland Journey from New York to San Francisco in the Summer of 1859.* New York: C. M. Saxton, Barker & Co., 1860.

Hendricks, Gordon. *Albert Bierstadt: Painter of the American West.* New York: Harry N. Abrams in association with the Amon Carter Museum of Western Art, 1973.

Hubbard, Fran and C. Frank Brockman. "Ice Cones and Frazil Ice." *Yosemite Nature Notes* 40 (April 1961): 16-18.

Huber, N. King. *The Geologic Story of Yosemite National Park.* Yosemite: Yosemite Association, 1989.

Hutchings, James Mason. *Hutchings' Tourists' Guide to the Yosemite Valley and the Big Tree Groves for 1877.* San Francisco: A. Roman & Co., 1877.

———. *In the Heart of the Sierras.* Reprint of 1886 edition. Lafayette, Calif.: Great West Books, 1990.

Huth, Hans. Yosemite, *The Story of an Idea.* Reprint of 1948 *Sierra Club Bulletin* article. Yosemite: Yosemite Natural History Association, 1984.

Johnston, Hank. *The Yosemite Grant, 1864 - 1906.* Yosemite: Yosemite Association, 1995.

———. *Yosemite's Yesterdays.* Yosemite: Flying Spur Press, 1991.

Jones, Holway. *John Muir and the Sierra Club: The Battle for Yosemite.* San Francisco: Sierra Club, 1965.

Jones, William R. *Yosemite: The Story Behind the Scenery.* Rev. ed. Las Vegas: KC Publications, 1992.

Julio, Richard. *Oh! Yosemite! Wonder 'Neath California Skies: A Picture of Yosemite in Verse.* San Francisco: Perlite Publishing Press, 1929.

King, Clarence. *Mountaineering in the Sierra Nevada.* Reprint of 1872 edition. Yosemite: Yosemite Association, 1997.

King, Thomas Starr. *A Vacation Among the Sierras: Yosemite in 1860.* Edited by J. A. Hussey. San Francisco: Book Club of California, 1962.

LaPena, Frank, Craig D. Bates, and Steven P. Medley. *Legends of the Yosemite Miwok.* Rev. 2d ed. Yosemite: Yosemite Association, 1993.

LeConte, Joseph. *A Journal of Ramblings Through the High Sierras of California.* Reprint of 1875 edition. Yosemite: Yosemite Association, 1994.

Matthes, François. *Geologic History of the Yosemite Valley.* Professional Paper 160. Washington, D.C.: U.S. Geological Survey, 1930.

McHenry, Donald. "Yosemite's Curious Frazil Ice." *Yosemite Nature Notes* 33 (April 1954): 38-39.

Merriam, C. Hart. "Indian Villages and Camp Sites in Yosemite Valley." *Sierra Club Bulletin* 10, no. 2 (1917): 202-205.

Morse, Cora A. "One Day's Worship." From *Yosemite As I Saw It* (San Francisco: San Francisco News Co., 1896).

Muir, John. *John Muir - To Yosemite and Beyond.* Edited by Robert Engberg and Donald Wesling. Madison: University of Wisconsin Press, 1980.

———. "Treasures of the Yosemite." *The Century Magazine* XL, no. 4 (August 1890): 487-488.

———. *The Yosemite.* Reprint of 1912 edition. Garden City, N.Y.: Doubleday and Co., 1962.

Nelson, Anton. "Five Days and Nights on the Lost Arrow." Reprint of 1948 *Sierra Club Bulletin* article in *The Vertical World of Yosemite,* edited by Galen Rowell (Berkeley: Wilderness Press, 1979.

Ortiz, Bev. *It Will Live Forever.* Berkeley: Heyday Books, 1991.

Osborne, Michael. *Granite, Water and Light: Waterfalls of Yosemite Valley.* Yosemite: Yosemite Natural History Association, 1983.

Reid, Don. *Yosemite Free Climbs.* 2d ed. Guilford, Conn.: Globe Pequot Press, 1998.

Reid, Don and George Meyers. *Yosemite Climbs: Big Walls.* Evergreen, Colo.: Chockstone Press, 1996.

Robertson, David. *West of Eden - A History of the Art and Literature of Yosemite.* Yosemite: Yosemite Natural History Association in conjunction with Wilderness Press, 1984.

Roper, Steve. *Camp 4: Recollections of a Yosemite Rockclimber.* Seattle: The Mountaineers, 1994.

Rowell, Galen, ed. *The Vertical World of Yosemite.* Berkeley: Wilderness Press, 1979.

Runte, Alfred. *Yosemite: The Embattled Wilderness.* Lincoln, Neb. and London: University of Nebraska Press, 1990.

Russell, Carl Parcher. *One Hundred Years in Yosemite.* Omnibus ed. Yosemite: Yosemite Association, 1992.

Sargent, Shirley. *Galen Clark, Yosemite Guardian.* Yosemite: Flying Spur Press, 1981.

———. *John Muir in Yosemite.* Yosemite: Flying Spur Press, 1971.

Snyder, James. "The Slide and Rebuilding of the Demolished Yosemite Falls Trail." *Yosemite* 47 (November 1981): 3-5.

Symmes, Harold. *Songs of Yosemite.* San Francisco: Blair-Murdock Co., 1911.

Taylor, Katherine Ames. *Yosemite Tales and Trails.* San Francisco: H. S. Crocker Co., 1934.

U.S. Department of the Interior, National Park Service. *Yosemite Valley Cultural Landscape Report.* Vol. 1. Project no. YOSE-504-15. Denver: U.S. National Park Service, 1994.

Whitney, J. D. *The Yosemite Book.* New York: Julius Bien, 1868.

photography

All photographs © by the individual photographers as credited.

Historic photographs courtesy of the Yosemite Museum Collection.

front cover and title page:
    © Michael Osborne
back cover: © Kirstie Kari
inside front cover: © Karl Kroeber
inside back cover: © Josh Helling
page 3: © Galen Rowell/
    Mountain Light
pages 4/5: © Pat O'Hara
page 6 (top): © Galen Rowell/
    Mountain Light
page 6 (bottom): © Karl Kroeber
page 7: © Kirstie Kari
page 8: from *The Geologic Story of Yosemite National Park*
    by N. King Huber, 1989,
    The Yosemite Association
page 9: © Josh Helling
page 10/11: © Karl Kroeber
page 12: © Josh Helling
page 13: Yosemite Slide Library
page 14: Yosemite Slide Library
page 15: Eadweard Muybridge and Party
    (photographer unknown)

page 30: © Michael Dixon
page 31: © Kirstie Kari
page 32: © Karl Kroeber
page 34 (top): © Guillaume Dargaud
page 34 (bottom): © Galen Rowell/
    Mountain Light
page 35: © Josh Helling
page 39 (top): ©Annette Bottaro-Walklet
page 39: Obata reproduction courtesy of
    the Fine Arts Museums of
    San Francisco, Achenbach
    Foundation for Graphic Arts

page 40 (upper left): © Al Golub
page 40 (lower right): © Kirstie Kari
page 40 (lower left): © Josh Helling
page 42: © Josh Helling
page 43 (upper left and right):
    © Kirstie Kari
page 43 (lower right): © Josh Helling
page 43 (lower left): © Al Golub
page 43 (center left): © Josh Helling
page 43 (center): © Kirstie Kari
page 44: © Josh Helling
page 45: © Kirstie Kari